JAYCEE
AND
OFFICER NINA
TALK ABOUT STRANGER DANGER!

DEDICATED TO:
MY CHILDREN, CONNOR, MADISON, AND JAYLEN
YOU THREE HAVE GIVEN ME MORE JOY
IN MY LIFE THEN YOU WILL EVER KNOW.
YOU WILL ALWAYS BE MY WHY.

LOVE,
MOM

BY: NANCY SWIDER

HI! MY NAME IS JAYCEE AND THIS IS MY MOM. SHE IS A POLICE OFFICER IN THE CITY WE LIVE IN. ALL MY FRIENDS CALL HER OFFICER NINA. I AM REALLY EXCITED BECAUSE TODAY SHE IS COMING WITH ME TO SCHOOL! SHE IS GOING TO TALK TO MY CLASS ABOUT STRANGER DANGER. DO YOU KNOW WHAT A STRANGER IS?

A STRANGER IS SOMEONE YOU DON'T KNOW, USUALLY AN ADULT OR AN OLDER KID, LIKE A TEENAGER. NOT ALL STRANGERS ARE BAD, BUT SOME ARE. WE ARE GOING TO TALK ABOUT HOW TO STAY SAFE IF A STRANGER APPROACHES YOU.

DON'T TALK TO STRANGERS! IF A STRANGER MAKES YOU FEEL UNCOMFORTABLE, IT'S OK NOT TO TALK TO THEM. MAKE SURE YOU CHECK WITH YOUR MOM, DAD, OR ANOTHER TRUSTED ADULT BEFORE YOU TALK TO SOMEONE YOU DON'T KNOW.

IF A STRANGER ASKS YOU A QUESTION, YOU DO NOT HAVE TO ANSWER. STRANGERS ARE NOT ALWAYS BAD, BUT SOMETIMES IT'S HARD TO KNOW IF THEY ARE NICE OR NOT. IT'S ALWAYS BEST TO CHECK WITH YOUR PARENTS BEFORE TALKING TO SOMEONE YOU DON'T KNOW.

DON'T TAKE ANYTHING FROM STRANGERS! MAKE SURE YOU CHECK WITH YOUR PARENTS OR A TRUSTED ADULT IF A STRANGER TRIES TO GIVE YOU SOMETHING LIKE A TOY OR TREAT.

TIPS FOR STAYING SAFE:

DON'T TAKE ANYTHING FROM STRANGERS!

TOYS

DON'T TAKE RIDES FROM STRANGERS! NEVER GET TO CLOSE OR INTO A CAR WITH SOMEONE YOU DON'T KNOW. MAKE SURE YOU DON'T TAKE RIDES FROM ANYONE, EVEN IF YOU KNOW THEM. CHECK WITH YOUR PARENTS FIRST!

TIPS FOR STAYING SAFE:

NEVER TAKE RIDES FROM STRANGERS!

ALWAYS CHECK IN WITH YOUR PARENTS BEFORE HELPING A STRANGER. IF A STRANGER ASKS YOU TO HELP THEM FIND THEIR LOST PUPPY, IT COULD BE A TRICK. THEY MIGHT BE TRYING TO GET YOU TO GO SOMEPLACE WITH THEM. ADULTS DON'T ASK KIDS FOR HELP, THEY ASK OTHER ADULTS. .

TIPS FOR STAYING SAFE:

CHECK IN WITH YOUR PARENTS!

MAKE SURE YOU CHECK IN WITH YOUR PARENTS BEFORE HELPING A STRANGER. IT COULD BE A TRICK!

HEY, YOU LOOK LIKE A HELPFUL KID. CAN YOU HELP ME LOOK FOR MY LOST PUPPY?

Lost Puppy!

Please Help!

I'M SORRY. I CAN'T HELP YOU NOW. I HAVE TO ASK MY MOM FIRST

11

CREATE A FAMILY PASSWORD! TALK TO YOUR PARENTS AND
MAKE A SECRET PASSWORD. DON'T SHARE IT WITH ANYONE ELSE.
IF YOUR PARENTS SEND ANOTHER ADULT TO PICK YOU UP, ASK
THEM FOR THE PASSWORD. ONLY GO WITH THEM IF THEY GIVE
YOU THE CORRECT PASSWORD.

CREATE SPACE BETWEEN YOU AND A STRANGER! IF A STRANGER APPROACHES YOU, MAKE SURE THEY AREN'T CLOSE ENOUGH TO TOUCH OR GRAB YOU. IF THEY KEEP COMING CLOSER, RUN. AWAY AND YELL FOR HELP!

TIPS FOR STAYING SAFE:
CREATE SPACE BETWEEN YOU AND A STRANGER

TIPS FOR STAYING SAFE:
CREATE SPACE BETWEEN YOU AND A STRANGER

IF A STRANGER GETS TOO CLOSE AND STARTS TO FOLLOW YOU AS YOU STEP AWAY, RUN! YOU CAN YELL THINGS LIKE "HELP! FIRE! STRANGER!" OR "GET AWAY FROM ME!" LOOK FOR THE CLOSEST TRUSTED ADULT AND TELL THEM WHAT'S HAPPENING.

15

BE AWARE OF YOUR SURROUNDINGS! WHEN YOU ARE IN PUBLIC, ALWAYS LOOK AROUND AND SEE WHAT AND WHO IS AROUND YOU. IF YOU SEE SOMETHING OR SOMEONE THAT DOESN'T LOOK LIKE IT BELONGS, TELL YOUR PARENTS OR A TRUSTED ADULT.

TIPS FOR STAYING SAFE:
BE AWARE OF YOUR SURROUNDINGS!

IT'S FUN TO PLAY AT THE PLAYGROUND WITH YOUR FRIENDS. JUST MAKE SURE YOU KNOW WHERE YOUR PARENT OR TRUSTED ADULT IS. IF YOU NOTICE SOMEONE ON THE PLAYGROUND THAT DOESN'T BELONG, GO TELL YOUR TRUSTED ADULT!

17

STICK WITH YOUR FRIENDS AND DON'T GO ANYWHERE ALONE IN PUBLIC. THERE IS SAFETY IN NUMBERS. IF YOU HAVE TO GO SOMEWHERE ALONE MAKE SURE YOUR PARENTS KNOW WHAT ROUTE YOU ARE TAKING AND LET THEM KNOW WHEN YOU ARRIVE TO YOUR DESTINATION.

DON'T WEAR YOUR NAME ON YOUR CLOTHING OR BACKPACK. YOU
DON'T WANT STRANGERS TO KNOW YOUR NAME. IF THE
STRANGER IS A BAD PERSON, THEY MAY PRETEND TO KNOW YOU
BY CALLING YOUR NAME.

21

TRUSTING YOUR GUT MEANS LISTENING TO THAT LITTLE FEELING INSIDE YOU THAT HELPS YOU MAKE DECISIONS. YOU CAN TRUST YOUR GUT TO GUIDE YOU AND HELP YOU CHOOSE WHAT FEELS BEST. TRUSTING YOUR GUT IS IMPORTANT BECAUSE IT KEEPS YOU SAFE AND HAPPY!

IF YOU MEET SOMEONE NEW AND YOUR TUMMY FEELS HAPPY AND CALM, THAT'S A GOOD SIGN. THEY MIGHT BE NICE AND SAFE TO TALK TO. BUT IF YOUR TUMMY FEELS FUNNY OR WORRIED, IT'S IMPORTANT TO BE CAREFUL. STAY CLOSE TO SOMEONE LIKE YOUR PARENTS OR A TRUSTED ADULT AND TELL THEM HOW YOU ARE FEELING.

23

THE BEST WAY TO STAY SAFE IS BY FOLLOWING THE SAFETY TIPS WE TALKED ABOUT. AVOID RISKY OR DANGEROUS SITUATIONS AND MAKE SURE YOU KNOW WHO YOUR TRUSTED ADULTS ARE.

SAFETY TIPS TO REMEMBER

1. DON'T TALK TO STRANGERS
2. DON'T TAKE ANYTHING FROM STRANGERS
3. DON'T TAKE RIDES FROM ANYONE UNLESS YOU CHECK WITH YOUR PARENTS
4. CHECK-IN WITH YOUR PARENTS BEFORE HELPING A STRANGER
5. CREATE A FAMILY PASSWORD
6. CREATE SPACE BETWEEN YOU AND A STRANGER IF THEY GET TOO CLOSE
7. BE AWARE OF YOUR SURROUNDINGS
8. TRUST YOUR GUT
9. STICK WITH A FRIEND
10. DON'T WEAR YOUR NAME ON BACKPACKS OR CLOTHING

FOR MORE INFORMATION AND SAFETY TIPS, VISIT:
WWW.TARGETED360.ORG

Made in the USA
Middletown, DE
25 September 2023

39037644R00015